TRACE & LEARN
CURSIVE WRITING
PRACTICE WORKSHEETS

Tons of practice exercises for your child to learn to write in cursive letters of the alphabet and acquire this endlessly rewarding skill in a few weeks with regular practice

By Shobha

ISBN-10: 0-9997408-0-6

ISBN-13: 978-0-9997408-0-4

Educators and teachers are granted permission to photocopy the designated reproducible pages from this book for classroom use only. No other part of this book may be reproduced in whole or in part, or stored in a retrieval system, or transmitted in any form or by any means, electronic, photocopying, or otherwise, without written permission of the publisher.

Copyright © 2018 Mathyz Learning
All rights reserved.
Printed in the U.S.A.

A a / A a	B b / B b	C c / C c
D d / D d	E e / E e	F f / F f
G g / G g	H h / H h	I i / I i
J j / J j	K k / K k	L l / L l
M m / M m	N n / N n	O o / O o
P p / P p	Q q / Q q	R r / R r
S s / S s	T t / T t	U u / U u
V v / V v	W w / W w	X x / X x
Y y / Y y	Z z / Z z	

Trace & Learn - Cursive Writing

Why learn cursive writing?

Motor skills, brain development and finesse

Print writing and cursive writing both require very different skill sets. Cursive uses the hand muscles in a different way. Moreover, it activates a different part of the brain which regular writing does not use. Analysis shows that learning to use cursive writing advances students' motor and visual skills. Exercising cursive handwriting augments and develops dexterity in our fingers and hands. These skills are the ones which are required of a dentist, artist, surgeon, and computer technicians. Cursive also promotes our hand-eye coordination and the linkage between our brain and hand. Even more remarkable is the fact that learning to use cursive writing productively affects mind development. Research also indicates that the kids who learn cursive in addition to manuscript writing have higher grades on both spelling/writing and reading exams, conceivably because the linked-up style of cursive writing compels writers to think of words as wholes rather than parts.

Students with learning difficulties

Students with learning difficulties e.g., dyslexia, may have a hard time with print writing since many of the letters are similar in appearance, especially b and d. On the other hand, cursive letters look very different from their print counterparts. This gives dyslexic students another choice, which can reduce their dyslexic impulses and make them more confident in their capabilities.

Cognitive skills and natural flow

The flow of cursive writing comes much more naturally to children as compared to print writing and engages greater cognitive skills. This cognitive development helps students reason, problem solve, conceptualize and make decisions as they get older. Cursive writing progresses fine motor skills such as coordination, development of muscles and hand-eye synchronization. Additionally, cursive writing's letter strokes aid in the eyes' left-to-right reading motion. Cursive is also productive for note-taking because a word in cursive is one entire block, instead of a stop-and-start series of strokes. This productive and efficient way of taking notes assists students in grasping information greater than typing. The phrase we all have been using, "Write it down or you'll forget it," is very true. Scientific studies on Neuropsychology suggest that the act of listening and handwriting links the verbal and spatial processing regions of the brain, strengthening memory. The overall excellence of syntax and writing is improved by this ability to reconstruct thought, ideas and lectures into written words, contrasted to those who type.

Other books from the author that might interest you:

BEGINNERS WORKBOOKS

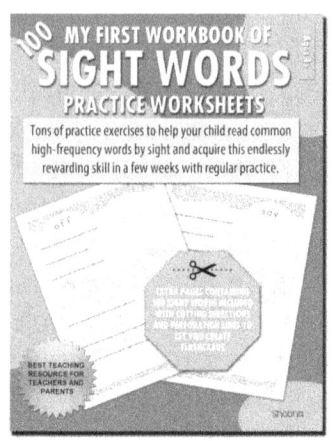  

TIME TELLING WORKBOOKS

BASIC MATH FACTS WORKBOOKS

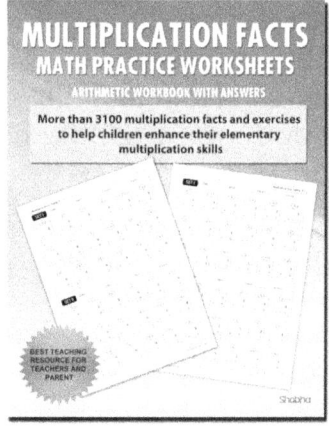 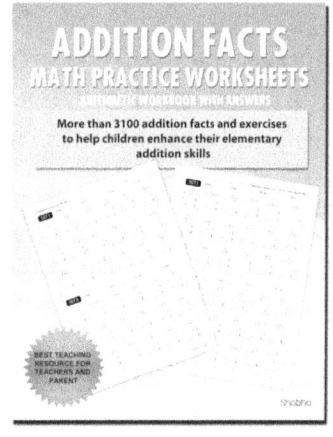 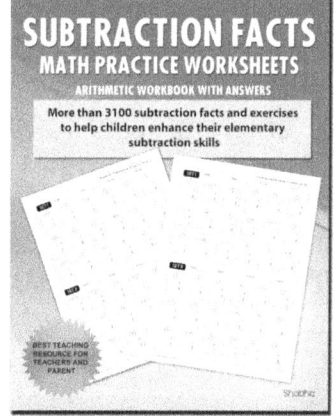 

Cursive Writing - Letter A

Trace the cursive letters. Follow the direction and sequence shown below.

Trace & Learn - Cursive Writing

Cursive Writing - Letter A

Trace the letters and then write on your own using cursive handwriting. Follow the direction and sequence shown below.

Cursive Writing - Letter B

Trace the cursive letters. Follow the direction and sequence shown below.

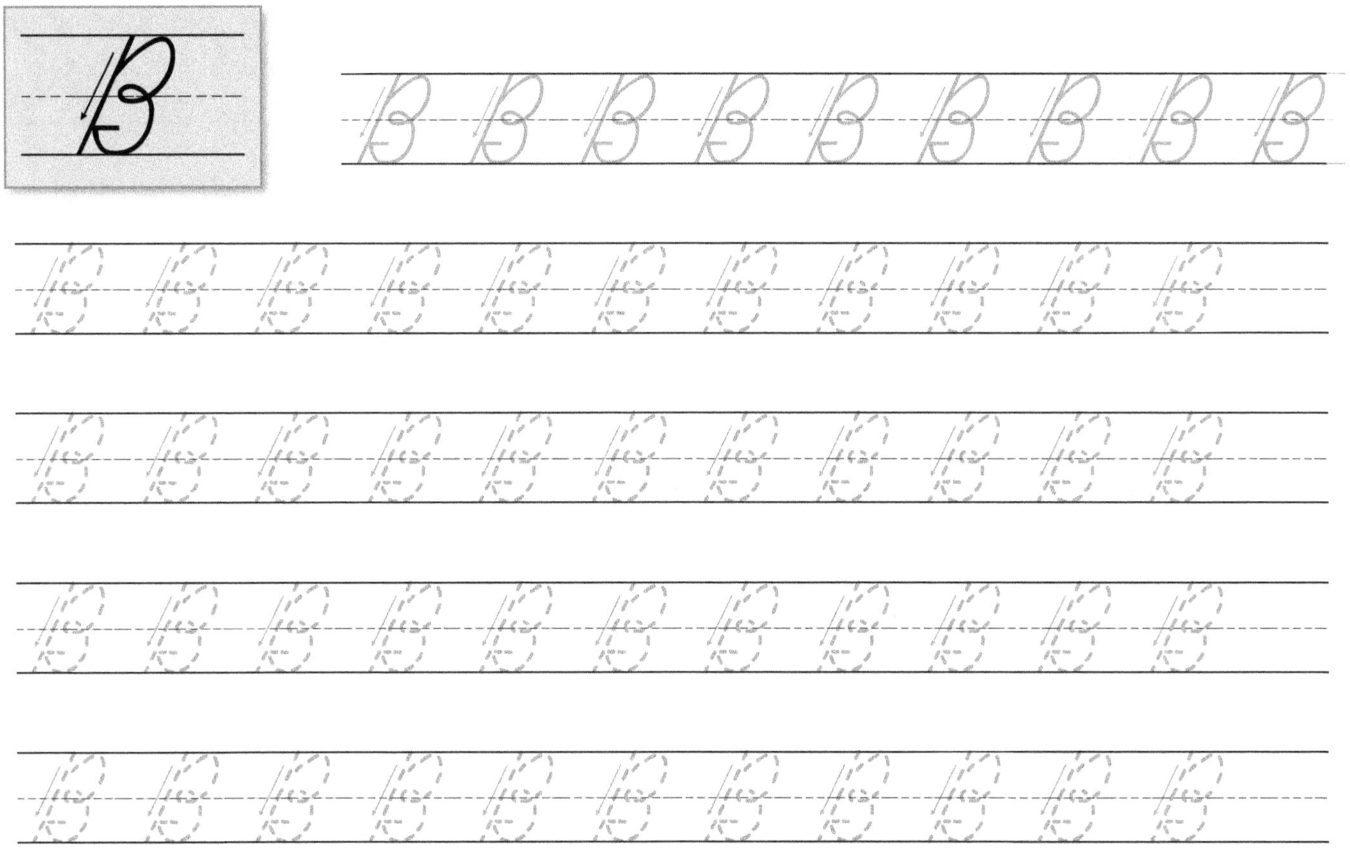

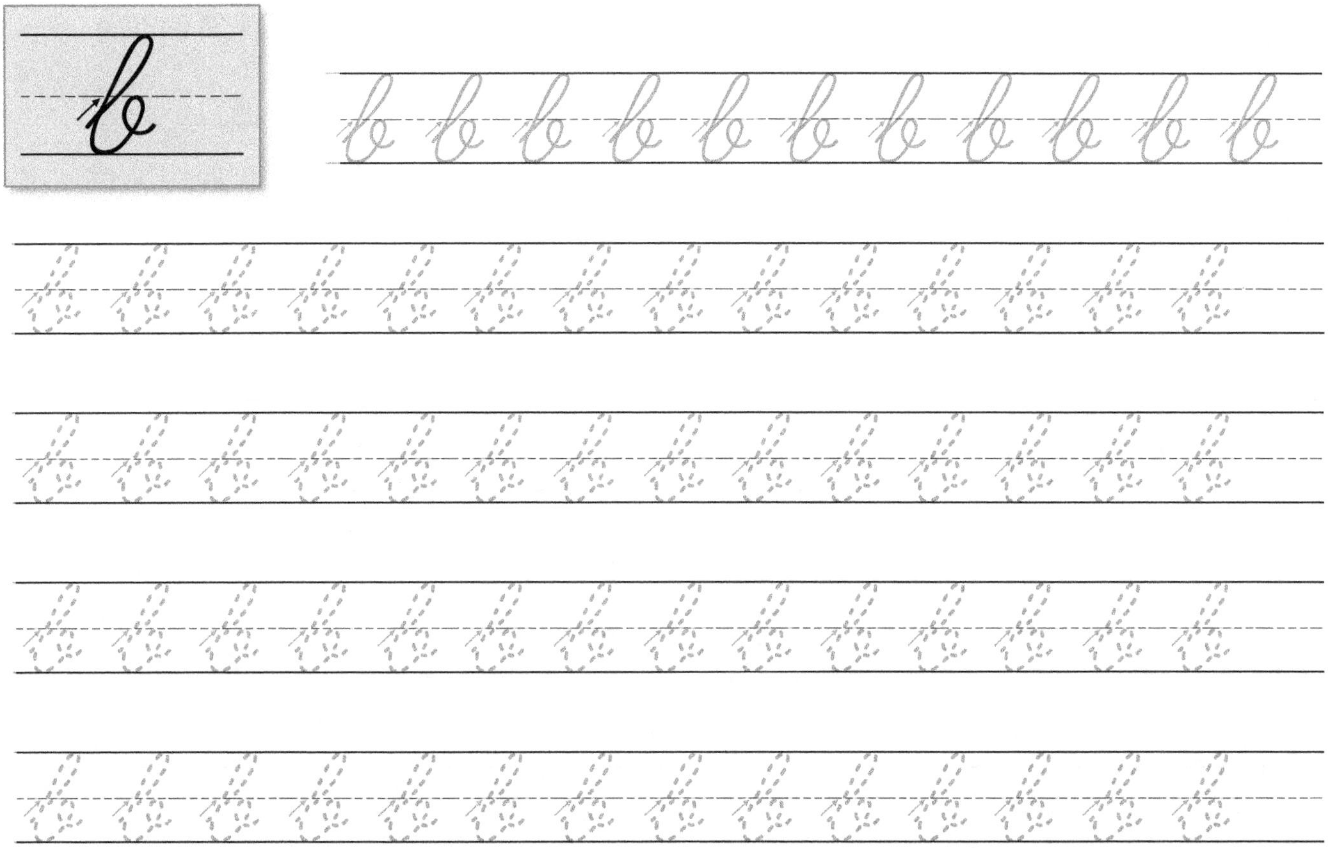

Trace & Learn - Cursive Writing

7

Cursive Writing - Letter B

Trace the letters and then write on your own using cursive handwriting. Follow the direction and sequence shown below.

Cursive Writing - Letter C

Trace the cursive letters. Follow the direction and sequence shown below.

Trace & Learn - Cursive Writing 9

Cursive Writing - Letter C

Trace the letters and then write on your own using cursive handwriting. Follow the direction and sequence shown below.

Trace & Learn - Cursive Writing

Cursive Writing - Letter D

Trace the cursive letters. Follow the direction and sequence shown below.

Trace & Learn - Cursive Writing

11

Cursive Writing - Letter D

Trace the letters and then write on your own using cursive handwriting. Follow the direction and sequence shown below.

Cursive Writing - Letter E

Trace the cursive letters. Follow the direction and sequence shown below.

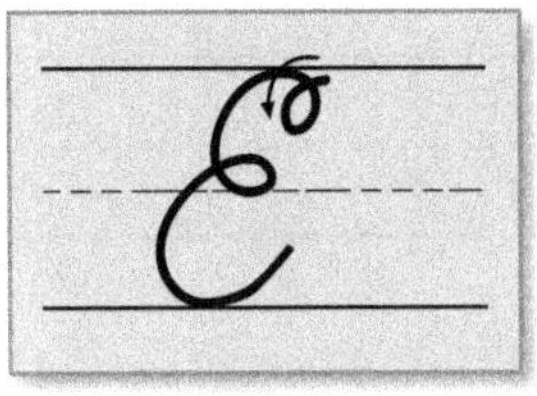

Trace & Learn - Cursive Writing

Cursive Writing - Letter E

Trace the letters and then write on your own using cursive handwriting. Follow the direction and sequence shown below.

Cursive Writing - Letter F

Trace the cursive letters. Follow the direction and sequence shown below.

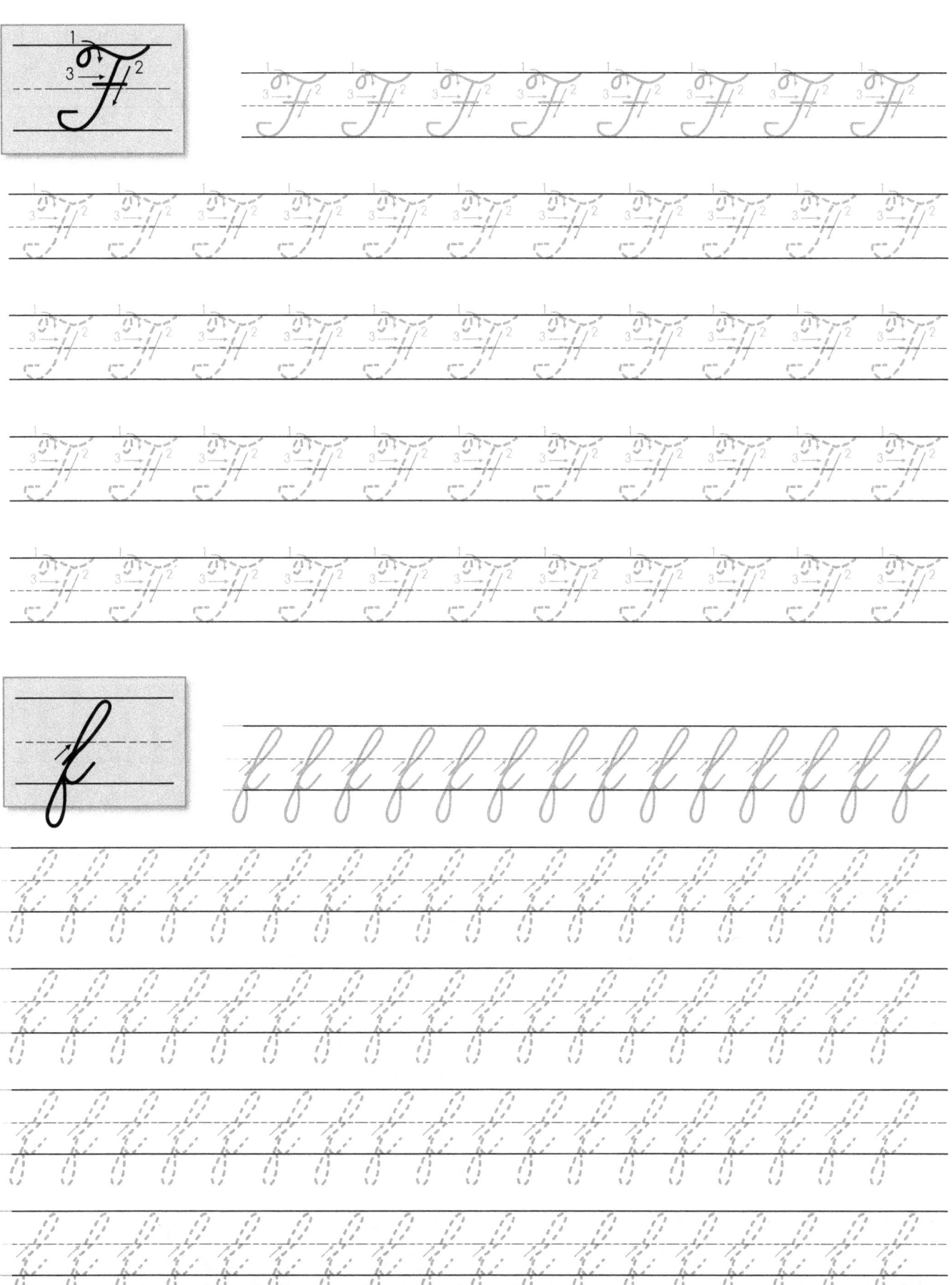

Trace & Learn - Cursive Writing

Cursive Writing - Letter F

Trace the letters and then write on your own using cursive handwriting. Follow the direction and sequence shown below.

Cursive Writing - Letter G

Trace the cursive letters. Follow the direction and sequence shown below.

Trace & Learn - Cursive Writing 17

Cursive Writing - Letter G

Trace the letters and then write on your own using cursive handwriting. Follow the direction and sequence shown below.

Cursive Writing - Letter H

Trace the cursive letters. Follow the direction and sequence shown below.

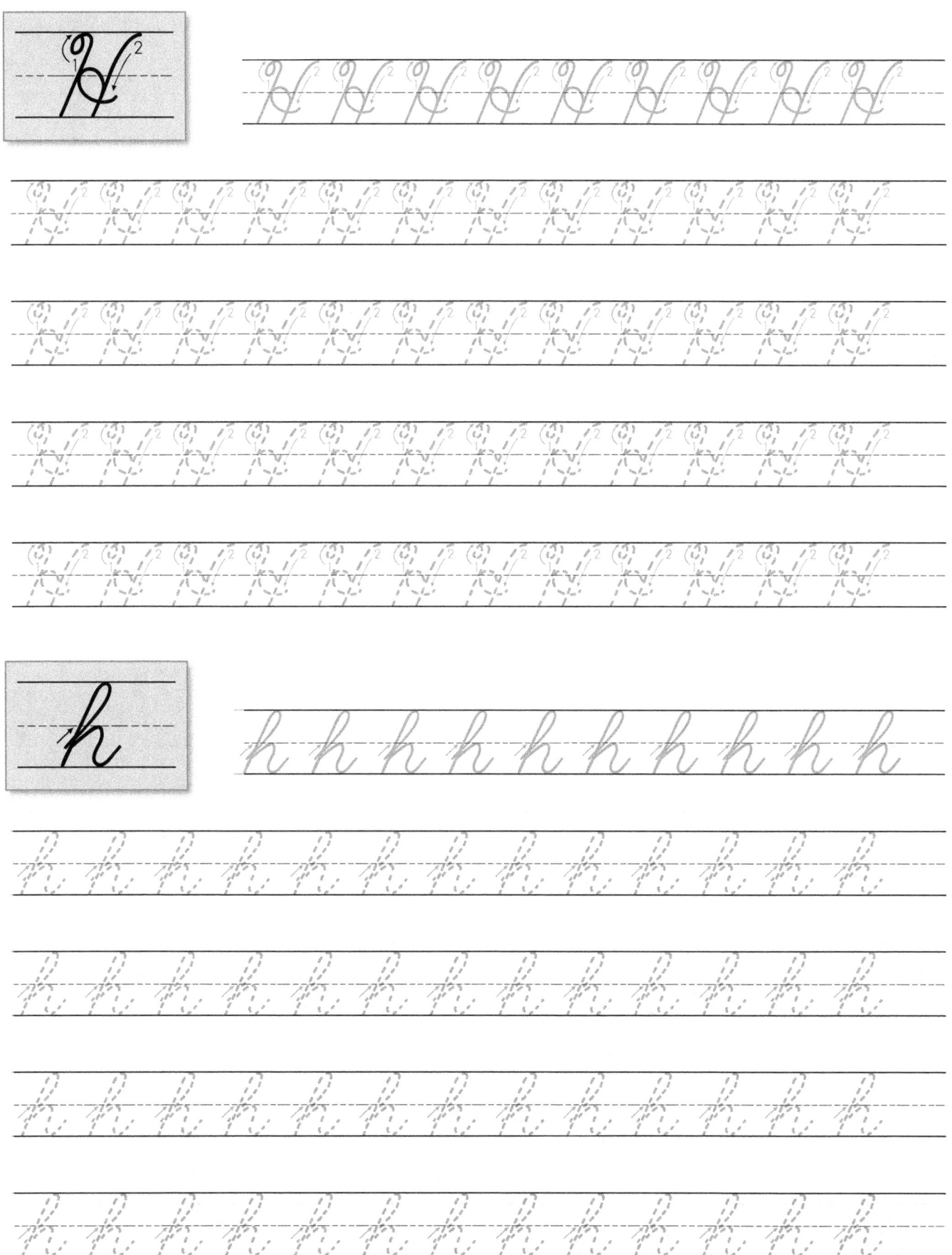

Trace & Learn - Cursive Writing

Cursive Writing - Letter H

Trace the letters and then write on your own using cursive handwriting. Follow the direction and sequence shown below.

Cursive Writing - Letter I

Trace the cursive letters. Follow the direction and sequence shown below.

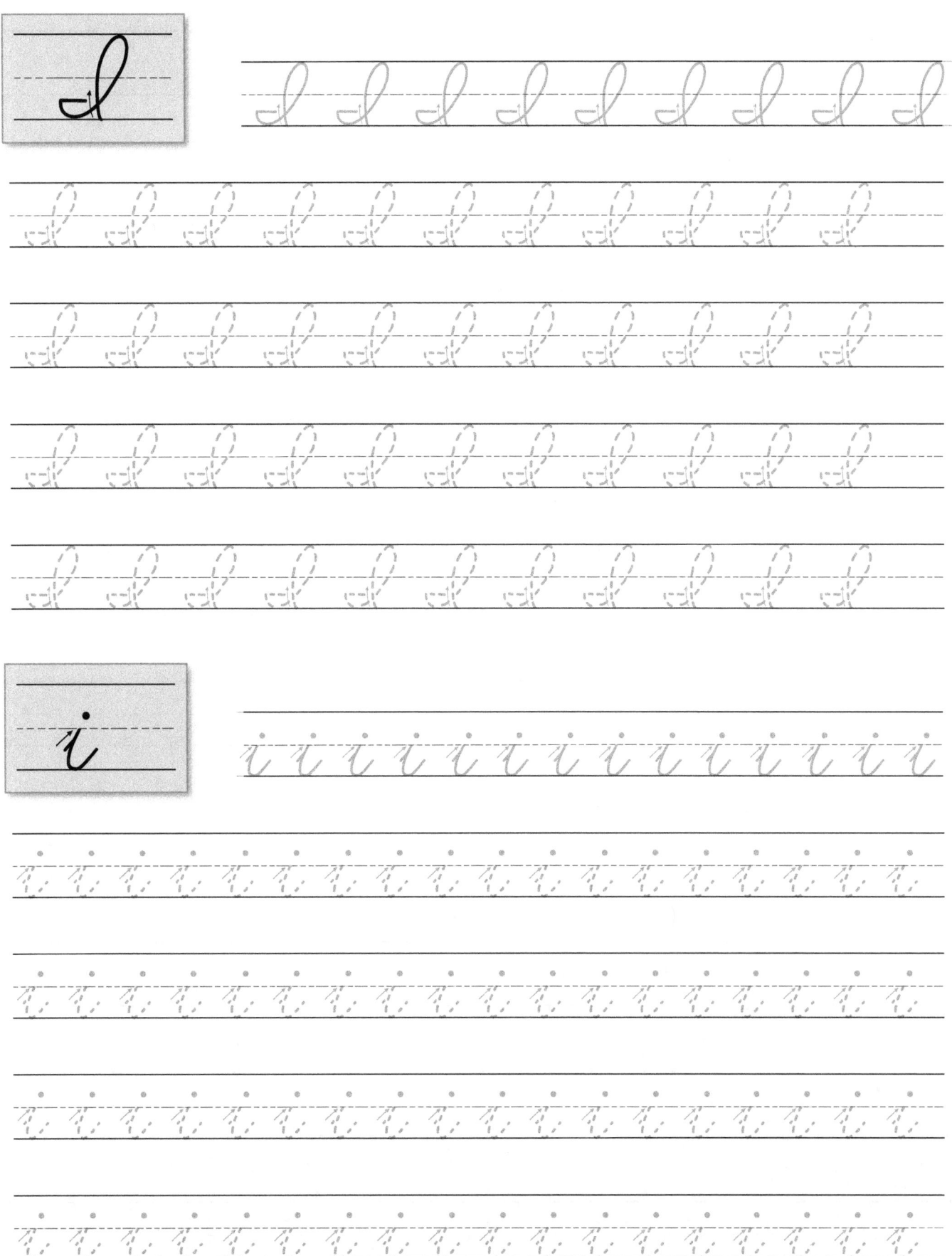

Trace & Learn - Cursive Writing

Cursive Writing - Letter I

Trace the letters and then write on your own using cursive handwriting. Follow the direction and sequence shown below.

Cursive Writing - Letter J

Trace the cursive letters. Follow the direction and sequence shown below.

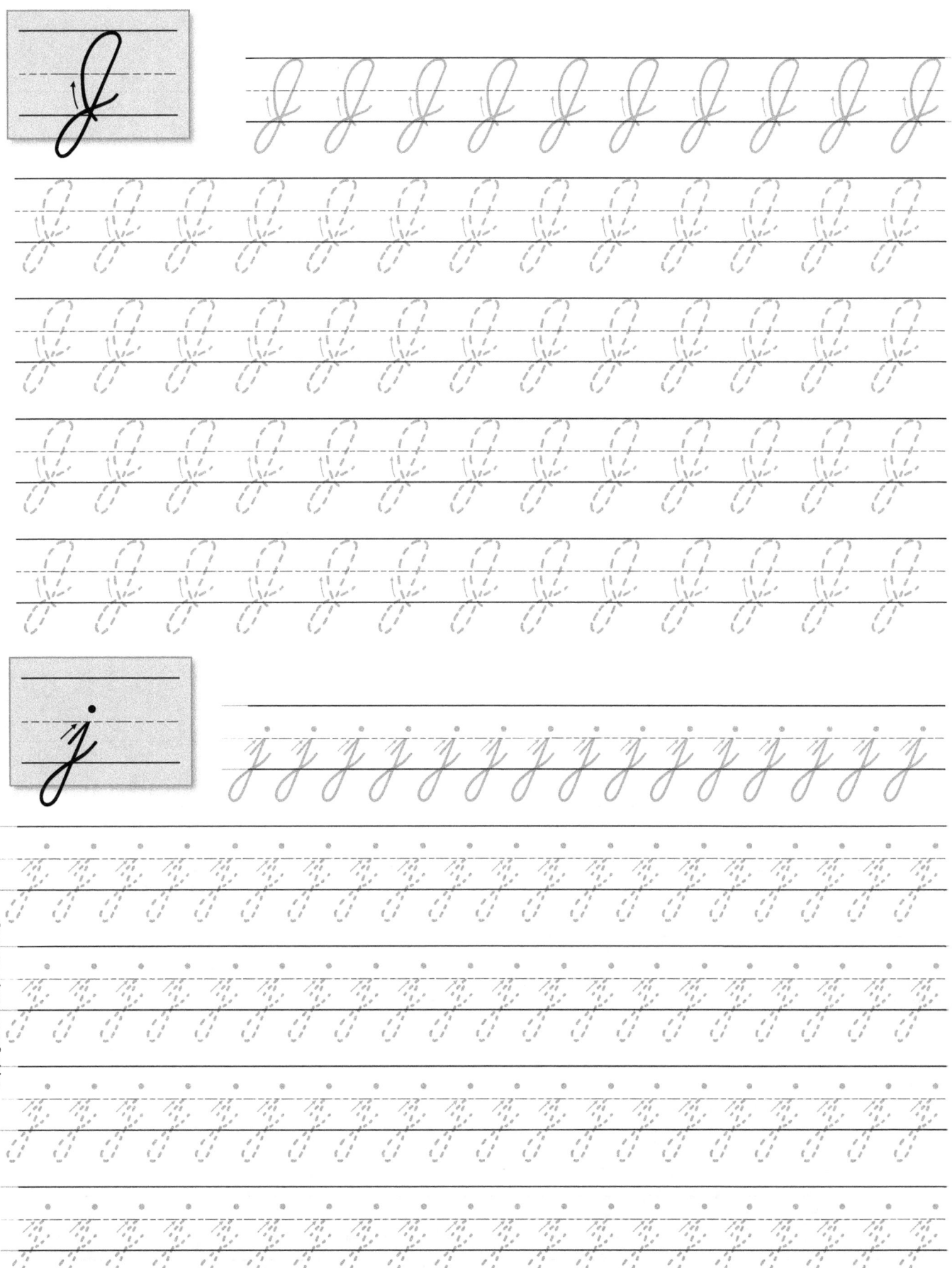

Trace & Learn - Cursive Writing

23

Cursive Writing - Letter J

Trace the letters and then write on your own using cursive handwriting. Follow the direction and sequence shown below.

Cursive Writing - Letter K

Trace the cursive letters. Follow the direction and sequence shown below.

Trace & Learn - Cursive Writing

Cursive Writing - Letter K

Trace the letters and then write on your own using cursive handwriting. Follow the direction and sequence shown below.

Cursive Writing - Letter L

Trace the cursive letters. Follow the direction and sequence shown below.

Trace & Learn - Cursive Writing

Cursive Writing - Letter L

Trace the letters and then write on your own using cursive handwriting. Follow the direction and sequence shown below.

Cursive Writing - Letter M

Trace the cursive letters. Follow the direction and sequence shown below.

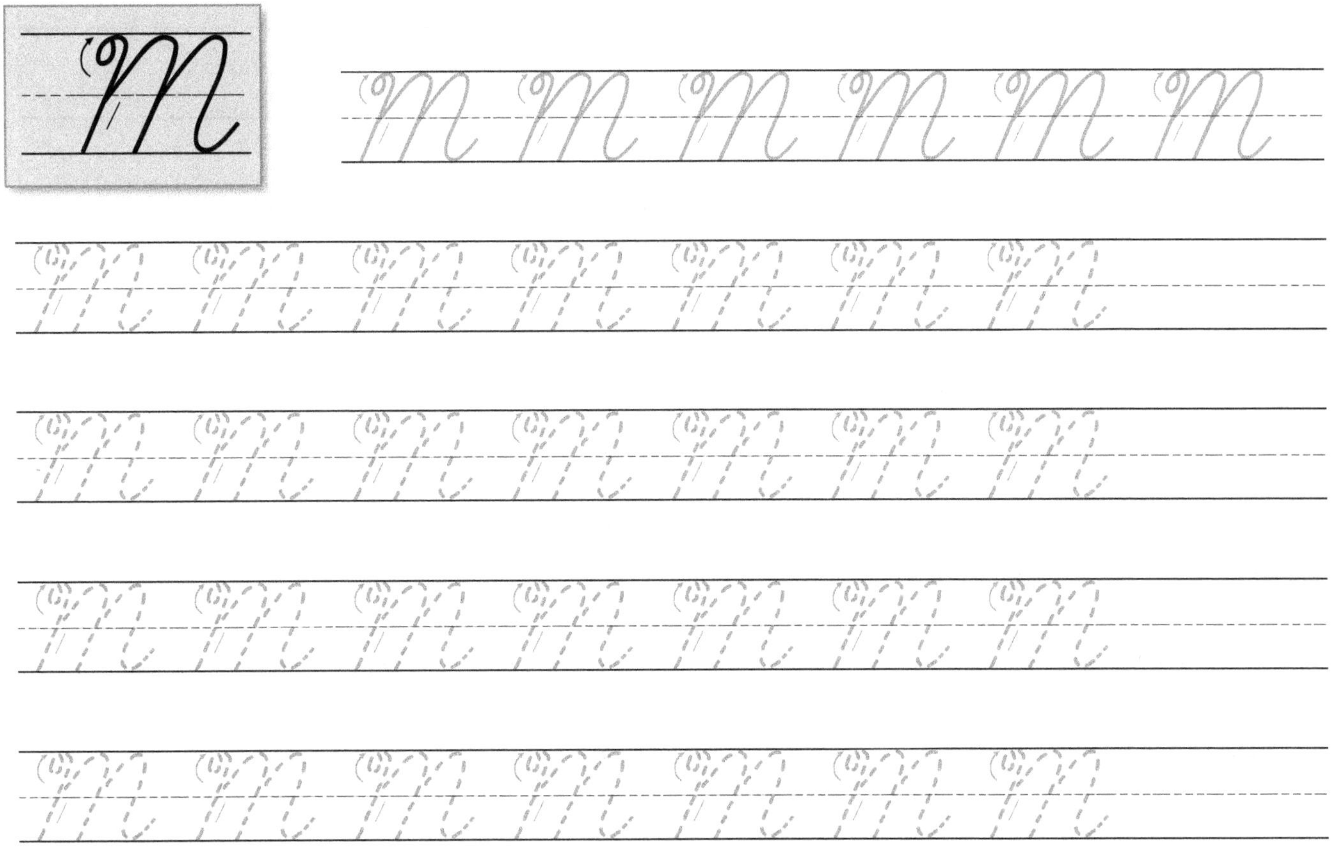

Trace & Learn - Cursive Writing

Cursive Writing - Letter M

Trace the letters and then write on your own using cursive handwriting. Follow the direction and sequence shown below.

Cursive Writing - Letter N

Trace the cursive letters. Follow the direction and sequence shown below.

Trace & Learn - Cursive Writing

Cursive Writing - Letter N

Trace the letters and then write on your own using cursive handwriting. Follow the direction and sequence shown below.

Cursive Writing - Letter O

Trace the cursive letters. Follow the direction and sequence shown below.

Trace & Learn - Cursive Writing

Cursive Writing - Letter O

Trace the letters and then write on your own using cursive handwriting. Follow the direction and sequence shown below.

Cursive Writing - Letter P

Trace the cursive letters. Follow the direction and sequence shown below.

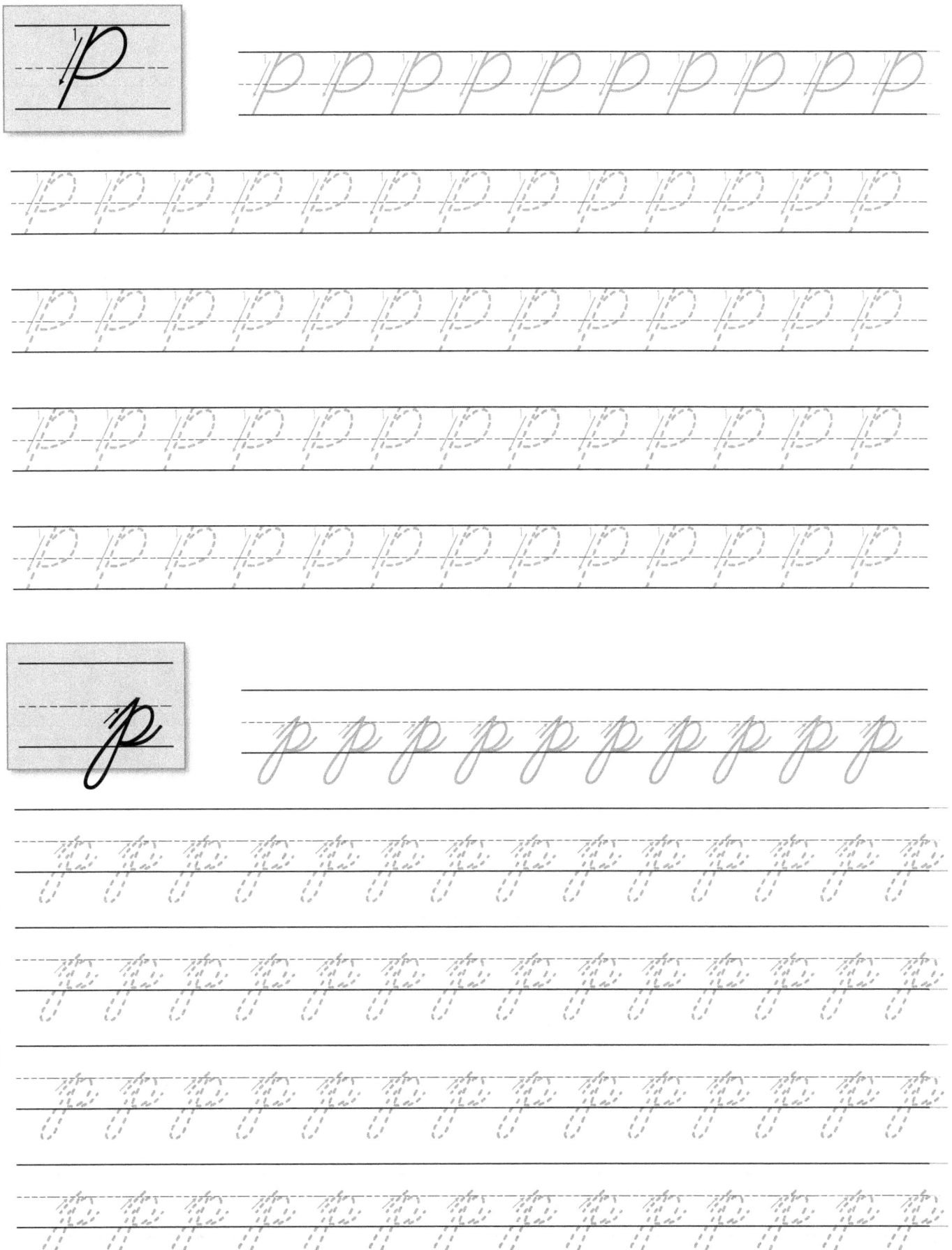

Trace & Learn - Cursive Writing 35

Cursive Writing - Letter P

Trace the letters and then write on your own using cursive handwriting. Follow the direction and sequence shown below.

Cursive Writing - Letter Q

Trace the cursive letters. Follow the direction and sequence shown below.

Trace & Learn - Cursive Writing 37

Cursive Writing - Letter Q

Trace the letters and then write on your own using cursive handwriting. Follow the direction and sequence shown below.

Cursive Writing - Letter R

Trace the cursive letters. Follow the direction and sequence shown below.

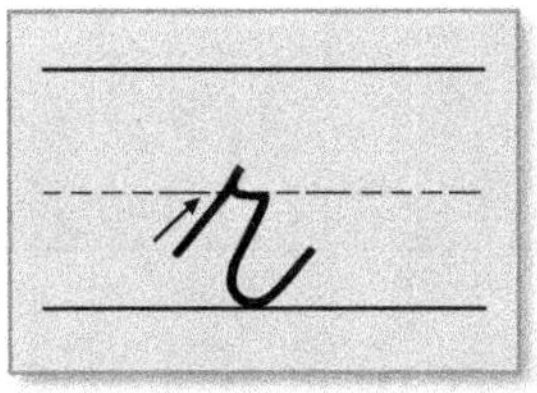

Trace & Learn - Cursive Writing

Cursive Writing - Letter R

Trace the letters and then write on your own using cursive handwriting. Follow the direction and sequence shown below.

Trace & Learn - Cursive Writing

Cursive Writing - Letter S

Trace the cursive letters. Follow the direction and sequence shown below.

Trace & Learn - Cursive Writing 41

Cursive Writing - Letter S

Trace the letters and then write on your own using cursive handwriting. Follow the direction and sequence shown below.

Cursive Writing - Letter T

Trace the cursive letters. Follow the direction and sequence shown below.

Trace & Learn - Cursive Writing

43

Cursive Writing - Letter T

Trace the letters and then write on your own using cursive handwriting. Follow the direction and sequence shown below.

Cursive Writing - Letter U

Trace the cursive letters. Follow the direction and sequence shown below.

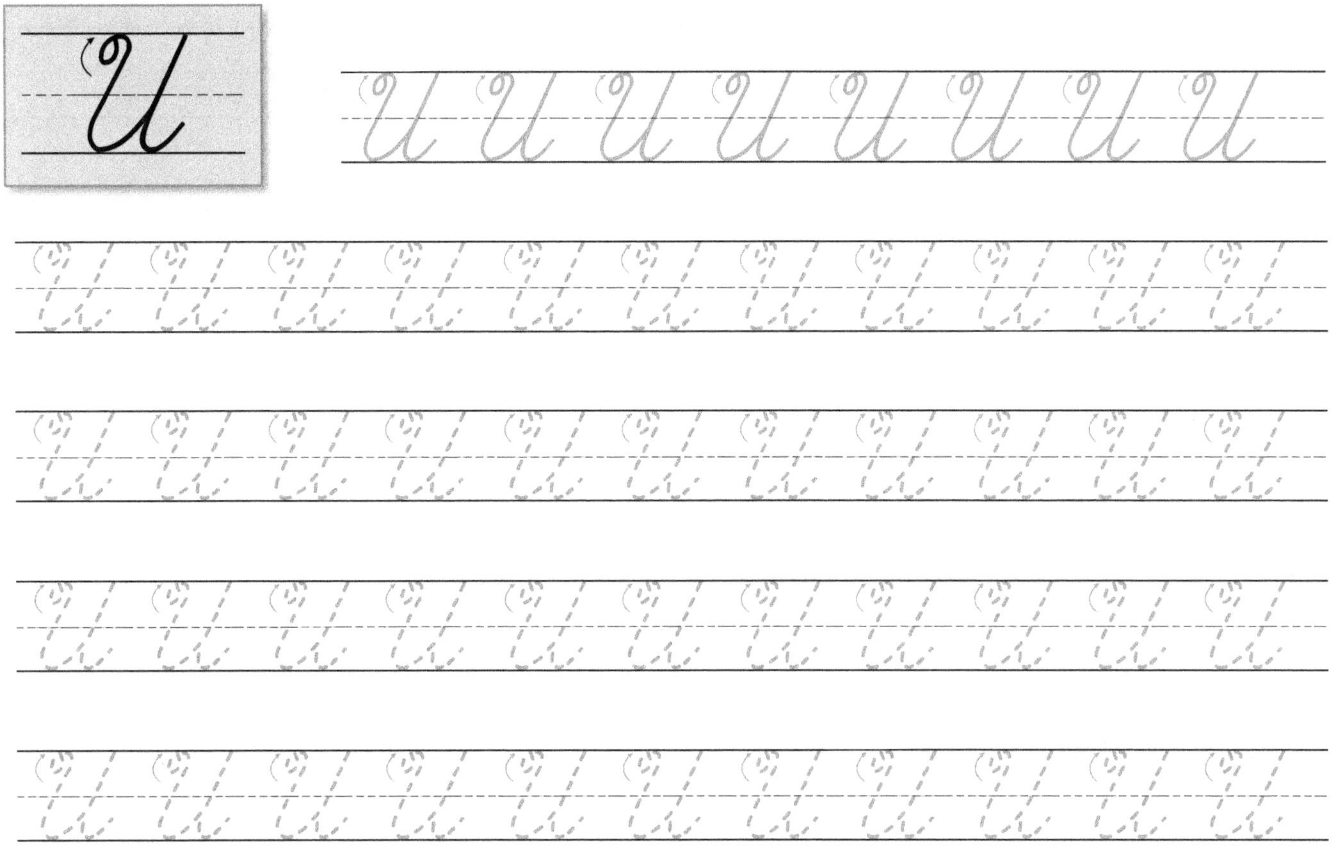

Trace & Learn - Cursive Writing

Cursive Writing - Letter U

Trace the letters and then write on your own using cursive handwriting. Follow the direction and sequence shown below.

Cursive Writing - Letter V

Trace the cursive letters. Follow the direction and sequence shown below.

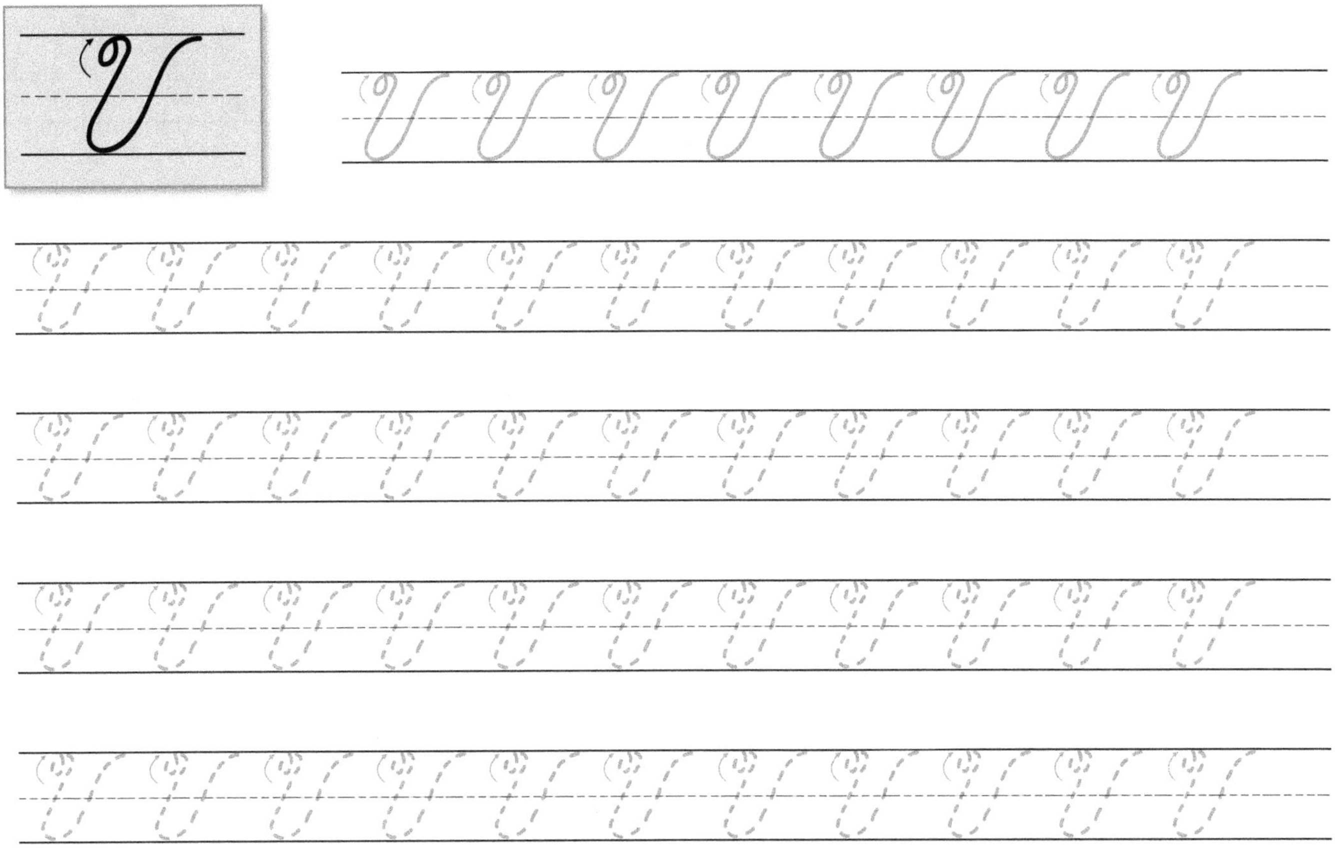

Trace & Learn - Cursive Writing

47

Cursive Writing - Letter V

Trace the letters and then write on your own using cursive handwriting. Follow the direction and sequence shown below.

Cursive Writing - Letter W

Trace the cursive letters. Follow the direction and sequence shown below.

Cursive Writing - Letter W

Trace the letters and then write on your own using cursive handwriting. Follow the direction and sequence shown below.

Cursive Writing - Letter X

Trace the cursive letters. Follow the direction and sequence shown below.

Cursive Writing - Letter X

Trace the letters and then write on your own using cursive handwriting. Follow the direction and sequence shown below.

Cursive Writing - Letter Y

Trace the cursive letters. Follow the direction and sequence shown below.

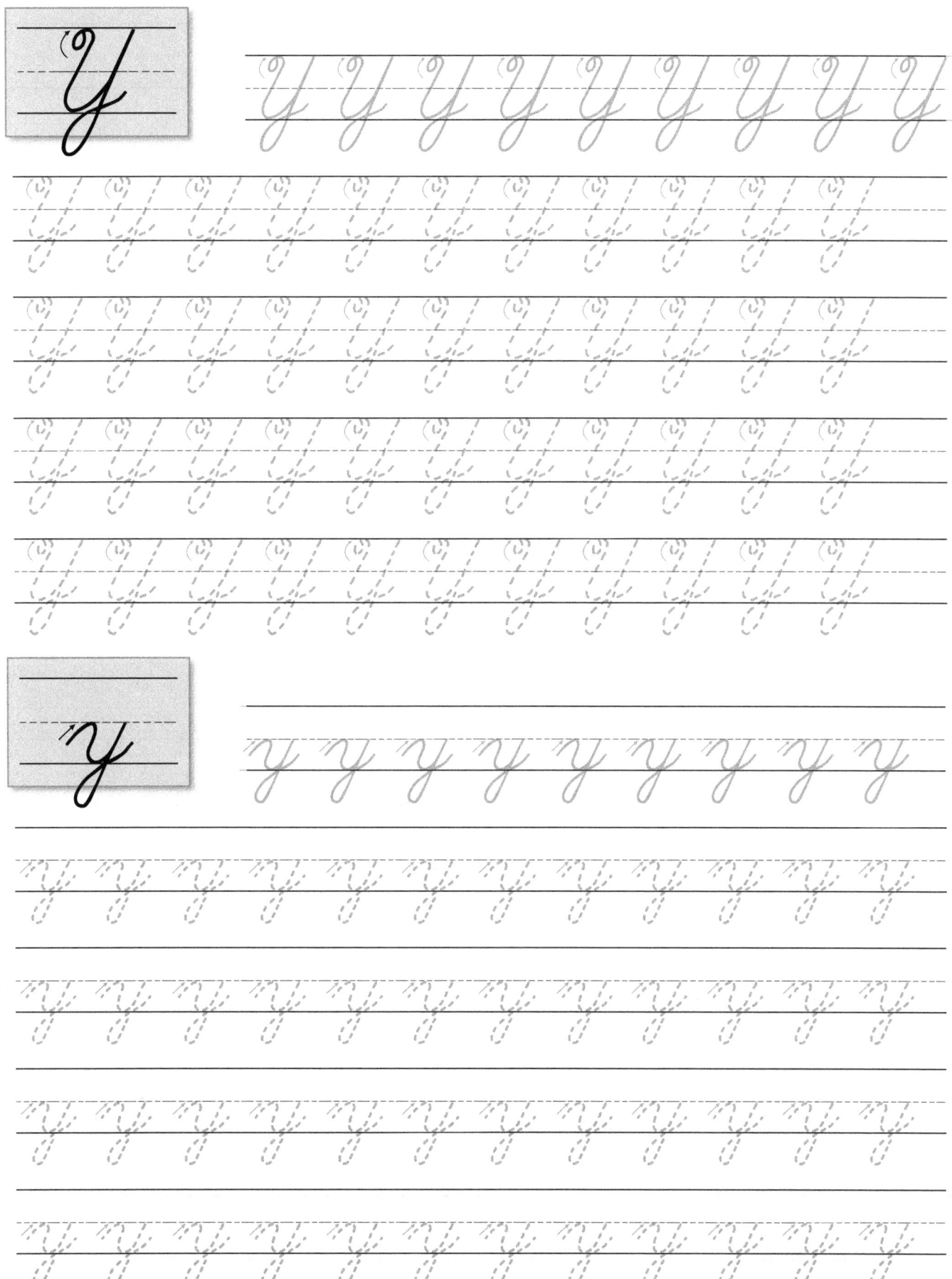

Trace & Learn - Cursive Writing

Cursive Writing - Letter Y

Trace the letters and then write on your own using cursive handwriting. Follow the direction and sequence shown below.

Cursive Writing - Letter Z

Trace the cursive letters. Follow the direction and sequence shown below.

Trace & Learn - Cursive Writing

55

Cursive Writing - Letter Z

Trace the letters and then write on your own using cursive handwriting. Follow the direction and sequence shown below.

Review: Cursive Letters A to Z

Write the letters using cursive handwriting. Follow the direction and sequence shown below.

𝒜

𝒶

ℬ

𝒷

𝒞

𝒸

𝒟

𝒹

ℰ

ℯ

ℱ

𝒻

Trace & Learn - Cursive Writing

Review: Cursive Letters A to Z

Write the letters using cursive handwriting. Follow the direction and sequence shown below.

G

g

H

h

I

i

J

j

K

k

L

l

Review: Cursive Letters A to Z

Write the letters using cursive handwriting. Follow the direction and sequence shown below.

M

m

N

n

O

o

P

p

Q

q

R

r

Trace & Learn - Cursive Writing

Review: Cursive Letters A to Z

Write the letters using cursive handwriting. Follow the direction and sequence shown below.

S

s

T

t

U

u

V

v

W

w

X

x

Review: Cursive Letters A to Z

Write the letters using cursive handwriting. Follow the direction and sequence shown below.

Y

y

Z

z

Practice writing cursive letters in the space provided below.

Trace & Learn - Cursive Writing

Cursive Writing - Practice Letters

Practice writing cursive letters in the space provided below.

A B C D E F G H I J K

L M N O P Q R S T U

V W X Y Z

a b c d e f g h i j k l m

n o p q r s t u v w x y

z

Practice by tracing the below pangram that uses all of the letters of the alphabet.

The quick brown fox

jumps over the lazy dog

The quick brown fox

jumps over the lazy dog

Cursive Writing - Practice Words

Trace the high-frequency words and then write on your own using cursive handwriting.

Like Like Like Like

like like like like like

Went Went Went

went went went went

Saw saw saw saw

saw saw saw saw saw

Must Must Must

must must must must

Want Want Want

want want want want

Trace & Learn - Cursive Writing

Cursive Writing - Practice Words

Trace the high-frequency words and then write on your own using cursive handwriting.

But But But But But

but but but but but but

Those Those Those Those

those those those those

jump jump jump

jump jump jump jump

Too Too too Too too Too

too too too too too too

Ready Ready Ready

ready ready ready

Cursive Writing - Practice Words

Trace the high-frequency words and then write on your own using cursive handwriting.

The The The The The

the the the the the the

Push Push Push Push

push push push push

That That That That

that that that that that

Your Your Your Your

your your your your

Each Each Each Each

each each each each each

Cursive Writing - Practice Words

Trace the high-frequency words and then write on your own using cursive handwriting.

This This This This

this this this this

Its Its Its Its Its Its

its its its its its its

House house house house

house house house house

Now Now Now Now

now now now now

Two two two two two

two two two two two

Cursive Writing - Practice Words

Trace the high-frequency words and then write on your own using cursive handwriting.

Pretty Pretty Pretty Pretty

pretty pretty pretty pretty

Please Please Please

please please please

Three Three Three Three

three three three three

They They They They

they they they they

Use Use Use Use Use Use

use use use use use use

Trace & Learn - Cursive Writing

Cursive Writing - Practice Words

Trace the high-frequency words and then write on your own using cursive handwriting.

Trace & Learn - Cursive Writing

Cursive Writing - Practice Words

Trace the high-frequency words and then write on your own using cursive handwriting.

Away Away Away

away away away

From From From

from from from from

Ate Ate Ate Ate Ate Ate

ate ate ate ate ate ate

Get Get Get Get Get Get

get get get get get get get

These These These These

these these these these

Cursive Writing - Practice Words

Trace the high-frequency words and then write on your own using cursive handwriting.

Does Does Does Does

does does does does does

Has Has Has Has Has

has has has has has has

When When When

when when when when

Who Who Who Who

who who who who who

Can Can Can Can Can

can can can can can

Cursive Writing - Practice Words

Trace the high-frequency words and then write on your own using cursive handwriting.

After After After After

after after after after

Some Some Some

some some some some

Were Were Were Were

were were were were

More More More More

more more more more

Was Was Was Was

was was was was was

Trace & Learn - Cursive Writing

Cursive Writing - Practice Words

Trace the high-frequency words and then write on your own using cursive handwriting.

Out Out Out Out Out

out out out out out out

Very Very Very Very

very very very very

Own Own Own Own

own own own own

Wear Wear Wear

wear wear wear wear

She She She She She

she she she she she she

Cursive Writing - Practice Words

Trace the high-frequency words and then write on your own using cursive handwriting.

Where Where Where

where where where where

Old Old Old Old Old

old old old old old old

There There There There

there there there there

Eat Eat Eat Eat Eat Eat

eat eat eat eat eat eat

His His His His His His

his his his his his his his

Trace & Learn - Cursive Writing

Cursive Writing - Practice Words

Trace the high-frequency words and then write on your own using cursive handwriting.

What What What

what what what what

One One One One One

one one one one one one

Have Have Have Have

have have have have

Live Live Live Live

live live live live live

See See See See See

see see see see see see

Cursive Writing - Practice Words

Trace the high-frequency words and then write on your own using cursive handwriting.

And And And And

and and and and and

Will Will Will Will

will will will will will

Than Than Than Than

than than than than

You You You You You

you you you you you

Are Are Are Are

are are are are are

Trace & Learn - Cursive Writing

Cursive Writing - Practice Words

Trace the high-frequency words and then write on your own using cursive handwriting.

Then Then Then Then

then then then then

Our Our Our Our Our

our our our our our

Her Her Her Her Her

her her her her her

With With With With

with with with with

Here Here Here Here

here here here here

Cursive Writing - Practice Sentences

Write the sentences using cursive handwriting.

The grass is greener on the other side.

God helps those who help themselves.

Don't judge a book by its cover.

Where there's smoke, there's fire.

Birds of a feather flock together.

A picture is worth a thousand words.

If you can't beat 'em, join 'em.

Two wrongs don't make a right.

Trace & Learn - Cursive Writing

Cursive Writing - Practice Sentences

Write the sentences using cursive handwriting.

Laughter is the best medicine.

You can lead a horse to water,

but you can't make him drink it.

Don't count your chickens before they hatch.

Beggars can't be choosers.

Absence makes the heart grow fonder

Honesty is the best policy.

The squeaky wheel gets the grease.

Cursive Writing - Practice Sentences

Write the sentences using cursive handwriting.

Actions speak louder than words

The enemy of my enemy is my friend.

Good things come to those who wait.

If you play with fire, you'll get burned.

When the going gets tough, tough get going.

Hope for the best, prepare for the worst.

The early bird gets the worm.

Two heads are better than one.

Cursive Writing - Practice Sentences

Write the sentences using cursive handwriting.

There is no such thing as a free lunch.

The pen is mightier than the sword.

Cleanliness is next to godliness.

When in Rome, do as the Romans do.

A watched pot never boils.

There is no time like the present.

If it ain't broke, don't fix it.

Better late than never.

Cursive Writing - Practice Sentences

Write the sentences using cursive handwriting.

Beauty is in the eye of the beholder.

All good things must come to an end.

Don't put too many irons in the fire.

You can't always get what you want.

Don't put all of your eggs in one basket.

Don't bite the hand that feeds you.

Fortune favors the bold.

Keep your friends close, and enemies closer.

Cursive Writing - Practice Sentences

Write the sentences using cursive handwriting.

Two wrongs don't make a right.

No man is an island.

Birds of a feather flock together.

There's no such thing as a free lunch.

There's no place like home.

Discretion is the greater part of valor.

Never look a gift horse in the mouth.

You can't make an omelet

Cursive Writing - Practice Sentences

Write the sentences using cursive handwriting.

without breaking a few eggs.

God helps those who help themselves.

Cleanliness is next to godliness.

Practice makes perfect.

Too many cooks spoil the broth.

Easy come, easy go.

Don't bite the hand that feeds you.

One man's trash is another man's treasure.

Cursive Writing - Practice Sentences

Write the sentences using cursive handwriting.

Necessity is the mother of invention.

A penny saved is a penny earned.

Familiarity breeds contempt.

Don't put all your eggs in one basket.

Two heads are better than one.

A chain is as strong as its weakest link.

If you want something done right,

you have to do it yourself.

Write the sentences using cursive handwriting.

A broken clock is right twice a day.

A friend in need is a friend indeed.

A little knowledge is a dangerous thing.

Better safe than sorry.

All work no play makes Jack a dull boy.

Don't put the cart before the horse.

Every cloud has a silver lining.

Great minds think alike.

Cursive Writing - Practice Sentences

Write the sentences using cursive handwriting.

Haste makes waste.

If you snooze, you lose.

It's no use crying over spilled milk.

It's not over 'till the fat lady sings.

Jack of all trades, master of none.

Look before you leap.

Measure twice, cut once.

Misery loves company.

Write the sentences using cursive handwriting.

Rome wasn't built in a day.

Slow and steady wins the race.

Still waters run deep.

Strike while the iron is hot.

The apple doesn't fall far from the tree.

There's no such thing as bad publicity.

Two is company, three is a crowd.

What goes around comes around.

Cursive Writing - Practice Sentences

Write the sentences using cursive handwriting.

What goes up must come down.

You can't teach an old dog new tricks.

You can't have your cake and eat it too.

You reap what you sow.

Don't cross the bridge until you come to it.

Where there's a will, there's a way.

Don't make a mountain out of an anthill.

An apple a day keeps the doctor away.

Cursive Writing - Practice Sentences

Write the sentences using cursive handwriting.

The cat is out of the bag.

Always put your best foot forward.

Don't bite off more than you can chew.

It takes two to tango.

Fools rush in where angels fear to tread.

A rolling stone gathers no moss.

Curiosity killed the cat.

Learn to walk before you run.

Cursive Writing - Practice Sentences

Write the sentences using cursive handwriting.

Money doesn't grow on trees.

It's the tip of the iceberg.

No news is good news.

Out of sight, out of mind.

Make hay while the sun shines.

Time and tide wait for no one.

The forbidden fruit is always the sweetest.

Cross the stream where it is shallowest.

Copy the following passage using cursive handwriting.

The United States of America was established on July 4, 1776 when the Declaration of Independence was issued, and is also called the USA, US, United States or sometimes America. The US is a diverse country with a multicultural society. The Mississippi and Missouri Rivers combine to form the longest river system in the US and the fourth longest in the world. The tallest mountain the US is Mt McKinley, located in the state of Alaska.

Cursive Writing - Practice Passages

Copy the following passage using cursive handwriting.

Officially, China is known as the People's Republic of China. China is in the Asian continent. China and Nepal are geographically separated by Mt Everest. China has many languages, including Mandarin, Yue, Wu, Minbei, Minnan, Xiang, Gan and Hakka. Beijing is the capital of China. Other major cities include Chongqing, Shenzhen and Guangzhou. The famous Giant Panda is found near the Yangtze River in China.

Cursive Writing - Practice Passages

Copy the following passage using cursive handwriting.

The Republic of India is the official name of India. India is in the Asian continent, and it is bordered by the countries of Bangladesh, Bhutan, Burma, China, Nepal, and Pakistan. Many different languages are spoken in India. The main ones are Hindi, Bengali, Telugu, Marathi, Tamil, and Urdu. The capital is New Delhi. Other major cities include Mumbai, Kolkata, Chennai and Bangalore. India's national symbol is the endangered Bengal Tiger.

Trace & Learn - Cursive Writing

Cursive Writing - Practice Passages

Copy the following passage using cursive handwriting.

England is one of the countries that make up the United Kingdom. England is bordered by Wales to the west and Scotland to the north. London is the capital. Other major cities include Birmingham, Manchester, Sheffield, Liverpool, Newcastle and Leeds. The longest river found entirely in England is the River Thames, it flows through London and is slightly shorter than the River Severn. Windermere is the largest lake in England.

Copy the following passage using cursive handwriting.

"Nihon" or "Nippon" which means "sun origin", is the Japanese name for Japan. Japan is part of the Asian continent. Surrounded by the Sea of Japan to the East and the Pacific Ocean to the West, Japan is an island nation. 6,852 islands form Japan. The highest point in Japan is Mount Fuji. Tokyo is the capital and also the largest city. Other major cities include Osaka, Nagoya, and Sapporo. Japan's official language is Japanese.

Cursive Writing - Practice Passages

Copy the following passage using cursive handwriting.

The French Republic is the official name for France. Latin word Francia, which means 'country of the Franks', is the origin for the name France. French is the official language. Paris is the capital. Other major cities include Marseille, Lyon, Lille, and Nice-Cannes. The famous Eiffel Tower in Paris was built as the entrance point for the 1889 World Fair. It is one of the most visited monuments in the world.

Cursive Writing - Practice Passages

Copy the following passage using cursive handwriting.

The Latin word 'australis', meaning southern, is the origin of the name 'Australia'. Canberra is the capital. Other large cities in Australia are Sydney, Melbourne, Brisbane, Perth and Adelaide. The 'outback', a desert area, covers much of the land. Australia is home to a variety of unique animals, including the koala, kangaroo, emu, kookaburra and platypus. Australia hosted the 1956 (Melbourne) and 2000 (Sydney) Summer Olympics.

Trace & Learn - Cursive Writing

Cursive Writing - Practice Passages

Copy the following passage using cursive handwriting.

The United Mexican States is the official name of Mexico. There are 31 states in Mexico as well as Mexico City, the capital. Mexico is home to over 30 UNESCO World Heritage Sites and is a popular tourist destination. Spanish is the main language spoken in Mexico. Mexican food is known for its range of flavors and spices, and popular dishes include tacos, burritos and enchiladas. The Football World Cup was hosted by Mexico in both 1970 and 1986.

Cursive Writing - Practice Passages

Copy the following passage using cursive handwriting.

The Russian Federation is the official name for Russia. Russia shares borders with many countries, including China, Ukraine, North Korea and Norway. Russia's official language is Russian but there are many other languages used in various parts of the country. Moscow is the capital and largest city. Other major cities in Russia include Saint Petersburg, Yekaterinburg and Novosibirsk. Russia is located across 9 time zones.

Trace & Learn - Cursive Writing

Cursive Writing - Practice Passages

Copy the following passage using cursive handwriting.

The Republic of South Africa is the official name of South Africa. South Africa has three capitals, Cape Town, Bloemfontein and Pretoria. Johannesburg is the largest city. Other major cities include Soweto and Durban. South Africa has 11 official languages, including Zulu, Afrikaans, Xhosa and English. South Africa is home to a wide variety of animals including giraffes, hippopotamus, leopards and lions. In 2010 South Africa hosted the FIFA World Cup.

Copy the following passage using cursive handwriting.

'kanata', which means 'settlement' or 'village' in the language of the indigenous St Lawrence Iroquoians, is the origin for the name Canada. Ottawa is the capital. Other major cities include Toronto, Montreal, Vancouver, Edmonton and Calgary. English and French are the two main languages spoken in Canada. Canada shares the longest land border in the world with the United States. The most popular sport in Canada is ice hockey.

Trace & Learn - Cursive Writing

Cursive Writing - Practice Passages

Copy the following passage using cursive handwriting.

In German, the name for Germany is Deutschland. Berlin, the largest city, is also the capital. Other major cities include Munich, Hamburg, Cologne, Stuttgart and Frankfurt. There are many national parks in Germany include the Bavarian Forest National Park, Jasmund National Park, Harz National Park, and the Wadden Sea National Parks among others. Germany has been home to famous composers such as Johann Bach, Ludwig van Beethoven and Richard Wagner.

Copy the following passage using cursive handwriting.

España is the Spanish name for Spain. Due to the early influence of the Spanish Empire, the Spanish language is spoken in many areas of the world. The largest city and capital is Madrid. Mount Teide is the highest mountain in Spain, and an active volcano. Spain includes a number of islands including Mallorca, Tenerife, Ibiza and Gran Canaria. Many can be found in the Canary Islands, an archipelago off the northwest coast of Africa.

Cursive Writing - Practice Passages

Copy the following passage using cursive handwriting.

The Italian Republic is the official name of Italy. Vatican City and San Marino are very small independent states located inside Italy. Part of Italy, Campione d'Italia, is located within the borders of Switzerland. Italy is in the continent of Europe. Countries that border Italy are Austria, France, Vatican City, San Marino, and Switzerland. Rome is the capital of Italy. Other major cities include Milan, Naples, Turin, and Palermo.

Practice Sheets

Practice writing anything on your own using cursive letters in the space provided below.

Practice Sheets

Practice writing anything on your own using cursive letters in the space provided below.

Practice Sheets

Practice writing anything on your own using cursive letters in the space provided below.

Practice Sheets

Practice writing anything on your own using cursive letters in the space provided below.

www.ingramcontent.com/pod-product-compliance
Lightning Source LLC
Chambersburg PA
CBHW060425010526
44118CB00017B/2366